A Guide for the Homeless:
Skills for Surviving the Streets

Index

Physical Needs

Shelter	5
Warm, dry, and cool	7
Food	10
Protection	12
Hygiene and Health	14
Money	23
Cars	28
Basic Gear	30
Resources	31

Psychological Needs

Positive Attitude	33
Dignity and Self-respect	33
Self-care and Love	34
Emotional Awareness	34
Getting enough sleep	34
Perspective	34
Anxiety	35
Future Moving	35
Choice	35
Victimization	35
Relationships	35
Boredom	35
Shame and Guilt	36
Suicide	36
Healing	36
Happiness	36
About the Author	39

Author's Books

A Different Road: From Bum to Mystic shares some of my experiences while homeless and traveling. My journey begins in prison and ends with a family and place to call home. Along the way I experienced death, healing, empowerment, & joy.

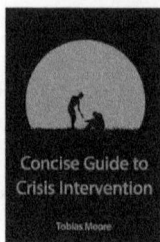

Concise Guide to Crisis Intervention talks about important skills needed to help those in crisis such as listening, recognizing signs, problem solving, knowing resources, inviting safety, increasing protective factors, safety planning, and teaching grounding, breathing, meditation, and other coping skills.

Crisis shares personal stories of my mental health struggles over the years, while offering different practices to help address depression, anxiety, PTSD, addiction, grief, loneliness, suicidality, and more.

Concise Guide to Consciousness follows consciousness down the phylogenetic tree from humans to singled celled organisms. The final chapter focuses on spirituality, meditation, and other conscious altering practices.

Physical Needs

Shelter
Warm, Dry, and Cool
Food
Protection
Hygiene and Health
Money
Cars
Basic Gear
Resources

Shelter

What is a shelter? A shelter or squat is a place that offers protection from weather, cold, wetness, and unwanted visitors. A good squat will also offer some permanence, be close to resources, and offer a place to use the bathroom: be that a toilet or some place to go without being seen or smelt.

Kinds of squats. Beyond homeless shelters, I've slept in the back of U-Haul trailers, in a RV lot, in the back of a city bus while on its route, trolleys, construction sites, abandoned houses, under houses, behind trashcans, under awnings, in bushes, on hills, inside trees, under evergreen trees, in recycle bins, under bridges, abandoned warehouses, drainage pipes, on roofs, on the beach, and a hundred other places: the possibilities are endless. Just be aware that it's illegal to trespass: do so at your own risk.

What makes a good squat?
- *Accessible*: Can you get to it easily?
- *Isolation*: Is it free of human traffic? Will people see you coming and going from it?
- *Protected*: Are you protected from rain? Wind? Animals? Cold ground?
- *Flat and spacious*: Is the ground flat and is there enough space?
- *Resources*: Is it close to food? What is the bathroom situation like?

Some places to look for squats
- Between buildings
- Behind bushes and walls
- Forests (check out Google Maps for locations)
- Under places like bridges and porches
- On top of business roofs
- Construction sites and abandoned houses
- Back of U-Haul trucks
- Tool sheds
- Bus stands
- Baseball dug outs
- Cardboard recycle dumpsters

Alternatively there are college parties, networking sites like couchsurfing.com, and city parks during the day. Some choose to sleep during the day because it's safer. While not always true, in general it is. It just sucks to stay awake all night and most resources are only open during the day.

I've found riding the bus away from large downtowns to be wise. The safest place to sleep is where no one else squats. Even walking for thirty minutes will usually get you outside of a smaller city's hub.

If you find a squat and then discover there is a lot of trash, graffiti, or other signs of traffic, find somewhere else. There is nothing worse than being woken up by someone kicking you or stealing your stuff.

What to do after finding a squat? Take care of it. Pick up your stuff. Don't leave anything valuable behind. Bring cardboard for the ground. Find a way to get to it without being seen or heard. Don't leave trash around. Pee and poo as far away as possible, or go in bottles, buckets and plastic bags and then carry it out with you. The key is to keep the squat as hidden and inconspicuous as possible. If no one knows you are there, no one will bother you.

Warm, Dry, and Cool

How to get clothes? Nearly every town, big or small, has resources for people in need. Churches and thrift stores are a great place to start. Some thrift stores and churches give away clothing vouchers. Ask and find out. If you're in a pinch you can raid free clothing bins: just know it's illegal and could get you arrested. As for plastic bags, most grocery stores have bag recycling boxes. Always have a handful of those. Buy some big bags if you can. If you are unable to buy them, a lot of places will probably give away a trash bag if you ask. I have received bags from the library and a fast food restaurant before.

7

How to take care of your clothes? Wrap clothes in those grocery store bags to keep them dry and make sure to wash or replace them regularly. Clothes can be washed in creeks, gas station bathrooms, park spigots, and laundry mats. Some laundry mats have sinks to use, but otherwise it's easy to panhandle enough money for laundry (see panhandling section for more information). If clothes are too funky or washing is just not an option you can simply replace them.

What you need to stay warm? The bare necessities are dry socks, layers, beanie or something else to cover the head, jacket, gloves, cardboard, and some form of plastic covering such as tarps, trash bags or plastic sheeting. Sweaters and long underwear are also really nice to have. When it comes to heat your three best friends are plastic, newspaper, and cardboard. Plastic works for trapping heat, placed on the ground to protect from moisture, or used as a tarp. Cardboard is great for placing on the ground. Not only is this helpful in softening the hard ground but it also acts as an insulator that prevents body heat from leaching away. You can also sleep inside a large cardboard fort. As for newspaper, you can stuff your clothes (shirts and pants) with crumpled newspaper pages or use it like a blanket. Other handy things to have are Mylar blankets which really keep in the heat and hand and foot warmers. Depending on where you are at you can have a fire or make a variant of the hobo heater with a large coffee can or something like it, toilet paper, and 70% isopropyl alcohol. Unroll and stuff the can with toilet paper until it's tightly packed (don't use cardboard roll, just the paper), then pour alcohol over toilet paper until it's pretty moist. Light it up and enjoy the heat. It burns clean, the can stays relatively cool, and it will stay lit for an hour or two. Just be aware and be safe: it is fire.

What you need to stay cool? Thin and loose clothing and a hat for shading. When the weather is extremely hot there are many places you can go: libraries, malls, transfer stations, Walmart, grocery stores, and fast food joints are a few city choices; while parks with shade, creeks, rivers, ponds, lakes, and caves are nice places to be around outside. When no shade is available you can create shade by tying up a tarp. Some other things you can do to stay cool are fanning yourself, soaking rags with water and placing over shoulders, neck, and head, misting yourself, eating lighter foods, and moving slower. Above and beyond anything else wear sunscreen and drink lots of water.

What you need to stay dry? A rain suit or poncho are ideal, otherwise having plastic sheeting or a tarp to cover up with and a 55 gallon trash bag with holes cut out for the arms and head will work. Some places to get out of the rain are libraries, malls, shelters, awnings, under overpasses and evergreen trees, fast food places, bus stops, baseball field dugouts, and any place you can hang up a tarp.

Food

Let's be honest, there will be days you go hungry. If you plan ahead and you make sure you know where to go, those days will be rare.

Food is often put in the back of the mind until you are hungry. To offset this it is helpful to have some go-to food. I always kept bread, peanut butter, and jelly packets from a fast food restaurant with me.

In most cities and some towns there is at least one place that feeds the homeless. The easiest way to find one is to ask another person on the streets. If that is difficult for you, then ask a postal worker, call police dispatch, look online, or go to where you get food stamps to ask. Check for DSHS office locations: https://www.fns.usda.gov/snap/apply. While at the food stamp office go ahead and apply for Medicaid: being homeless qualifies you.

Places that offer food:
- *Food banks*: Food boxes (usually with some fresh stuff to eat right away)
- *Soup kitchens*: There are many different organizations that feed the homeless.
- *Churches*: Even when churches are not actively feeding, I have gone to church and told a pastor what was going on and by the end of service I had three families wanting to help.

Other Sources

- *Left overs*: One of the easiest ways to eat is to hangout near a restaurant that you like and wait for people to come out with their leftovers and then ask, "Spare some leftovers?" More times than not you'll score some food. Just a word of warning, don't frequent the same restaurant too often and don't attract the attention of those going in because you will be chased off.

- *Dumpster diving*: Times are changing with this one. When I lived on the streets practically every place threw out their stuff for the picking. Now-a-days most grocery stores have the Dragon (garbage compactor). Even so, smaller grocery stores still have the classic dumpster. When it comes to dumpster diving only take what is on top and make sure that it is wrapped up and not open. It doesn't take much to get sick, so be careful. Keep in mind dumpster diving is considered trespassing in some places.

- *Fast food*: At the end of the night fast food places throw away a lot of stuff. It's a hit or miss if the food's good – sometimes it is just cold and nasty while other times it's covered in coffee grounds, soda, or some other disgusting substance.

- *Work trade*: This one might seem weird, but I've walked into mom and pop restaurants and asked to work in exchange for a meal: it works. One time I even went to Subway and mopped floors with a friend for a sub.

Protection

Things to help keep you safe

- *Common sense*: Take a moment and think: what makes sense? Most problems can be avoided if you think before acting.
- *Awareness*: Be aware of your environment, the people around you, and the choices you make.
- *Vigilance*: Don't become complacent, don't let your guard down, constantly be aware.
- *Trusting the gut*: If something inside you is telling you not to go down there, to watch out for this person, to not sleep there or eat that, if your gut is telling you something is wrong - listen to it. It is better to err on the side of safety than to put yourself in dangerous situations. The more you pay attention to your instincts, the easier it will be to survive the streets.
- *Not setting yourself up*: Don't put yourself in situations that will invite trouble. If you know some people are dangerous, don't go around them. If you know it takes a certain amount of time to get to your squat, don't wait until it's too late to get there. The more aware you are, the less you'll set yourself up.
- *Learning from your mistakes*: When something unwanted happens, learn from it. How did it happen? What could you do different? What signs were there? Ask yourself these and similar questions and then answer them. Now you know.
- *Not being predictable*: Don't walk straight to your squat the same way every night. Come at it

from different directions and times. Also try to have more than one squat so that you can split your time between them.

- *Get a free phone*: https://www.freegovernmentcellphones.net/states

- *Stay away from erratic people*: Be aware and don't put yourself in unsafe situations. If you see someone screaming, hitting things, staring down at people, or just looking for trouble, cross the street, go another way, or pass by in a crowd.

- *Don't flaunt*: If you don't want to get jumped and your stuff stolen, then don't flaunt your stuff.

- *Don't leave behind things you want*: If you have a good squat it's sometimes nice to leave behind a few things, but never, under any circumstance, leave behind things you want to keep. Even the best squat can be found. Always keep your valuables with you.

- *Mind your own business*: There is no quicker way to get in trouble than sticking your nose in other people's business.

- *Sleeping*: Keep your most prized possessions in the sleeping bag with you while using your backpack/bag as a pillow.

- *Avoid* violence, conflict, and confrontation as much as possible. If you find yourself caught in it, try to run. If that does not work, try distraction or manipulation, and if that doesn't work, fight with all you have while screaming fire or something like that until you get someone's attention or create a chance for you to run away. And remember, your life is worth more than any possession. Throw your stuff in their face and run if you have to.

- *Stay away from sick people:* It really sucks to get sick, especially when you are homeless. What normally takes a week or two to get over, sometimes stays for months on the streets. If you're seeing sick people, avoid them. Make sure to use hand sanitizer often. Drink lots of water. And if you're unable to avoid being around sickness, wear a mask or some fabric over your mouth and nose. If you do get sick and need help, go to the hospital. You'll have a few hours of rest in a safe and dry place and you'll get medication if needed. Use this time to figure out what you're going to do. Also, be nice to the hospital staff and they will treat you nicely.

- *Contact with other homeless:* It's a mistake to think just because someone is homeless that they are violent, drug addicted, or mentally unstable. Homeless people are just like everyone else. Even so, stuff does happen. While it is inevitable you will have contact with other people on the streets, you don't have to stay around after accessing resources.

- *Contact with law enforcement:* It's going to happen. The best thing you can do is avoid things that will put you on their radar. When you do have contact, be respectful. Don't be belligerent, insulting, or threatening.

Hygiene and Health

Hygiene is usually not on the top of the list when it comes to living on the streets, but I can tell you from experience it is something you definitely want to pay attention to. For years I didn't brush my teeth and now they're falling out. I've seen people get scabies so bad they got staph infection, people with giardia shitting down their leg, and a common cold that led into pneumonia. Learn to take care of the basics and make sure to do simple hygiene. It's not always easy, but a good habit will ultimately save you a lot of trouble later on.

Another thing to consider is how much easier it is to exist in society when you're presentable. If you are dirty and smelly, people will notice you. By taking care of your hygiene and presentation, you will avoid a lot of attention.

Simple hygiene techniques and healthy actions
- Always have hygiene stuff with you (soap, toothbrush, toothpaste, comb, body powder, deodorant, razor, nail clippers, and so on).
- Air feet out one or more times a day (take off shoes and socks).
- Drink water throughout the day.
- Stop or lessen smoking, drinking, and drug intake when you can.
- Have something to wipe with (get some toilet paper from a bathroom).
- Get Medicaid, get a checkup and go to the dentist.

- Keep the hands clean: hand sanitizer or alcohol wipes are really good to keep around.
- Brush your teeth at least once a day.
- Dedicate a few minutes of your day to checking over the body. Pay attention to your body and see if anything is off. If there is, do something about it.
- Wash regularly. Ways to wash-up:
  - Public bathrooms
  - Streams, rivers, ponds, and lakes
  - Water bottles and rags
  - Baby wipes
  - Places to shower
    - Beaches
    - Gyms
    - College campuses
    - Public pools
    - Motels/Hotels (in the morning maids usually open a few doors at a time, go to the one furthest from the maid and be quick. Be aware that this is trespassing and you do so at your own risk)
    - Shelters
    - Local charity organizations
    - National Parks and camp grounds
    - Night sprinklers at golf courses and neighborhoods
    - Some churches
    - If you're camping, solar shower

- Helpful strangers getting us a motel room or taking us home for the night

When taking a shower in public bathrooms it's important to protect your feet from athletes-foot or other infections. Having cheap flip-flops from the Dollar Store is perfect, if not, at least cover your feet with a plastic bag and don't forget to clean your feet at the end of your shower.

Disclaimer: The following information is not meant to substitute the medical advice of a licensed physician. Please refer to licensed physician for medical advice. Use at your own risk.

Urinary Tract Infections (UTI)

Symptoms
- Need to pee more often, even if only a small amount comes out
- Irritation and/or pain around bladder and the pee tube (urethra) such as burning or itchy feeling near the top of urethra
- Changes in characteristics/quality of pee such as cloudy, dark, red tinted, strange-smelling, of different amounts
- Discomfort in lower back
- Chills
- Fatigue
- Experiencing deliriums for the first time or a noticeable increase of agitation, restlessness, hallucinations, and delusions

- Drink a lot of water.
- Wash genitals area with baby wipe daily.
- Try not to hold pee too long – pee often.

Treatment

- Load up on vitamin C which helps acidify urine.
- Take uva ursi or oregano tincture and/or consume crushed garlic three times a day when you notice initial symptoms. If symptoms persist for more than a week go to the hospital and get antibiotics.

Scabies

- *Symptoms*: Extremely itchy pimple-like rash between fingers, folds of skin, waistline, navel, breasts and genitals, head, neck, face, palms, and soles of the feet. Sores can be scaled or blistered, and they are usually clustered together. There might be tiny burrows under skin as well.
- *Prevention*: Avoid people infected at all cost. Clean public toilet seats and/or use paper seat cover. Be careful who you sleep with.
- *Treatment*: Clean yourself and your belongings. Eat lots and lots of garlic until it is oozing from your skin. This makes your flesh inhospitable. Apply either anise, neem, or tansy oil over infected areas. If treatment is not helping go to the hospital. Be careful where you sit to make sure you don't spread them to others. To deal with the itchiness use Calamine, Afterbite,

vinegar, honey, vapor rub, deodorant, or thyme essential oil. You can get little packets of honey and vinegar from some fast food restaurants.

Chiggers

- *Symptoms*: Small red spots with a slight bump usually found in the folds of skin and where clothing is tight like waistband, armpits, crotch, and behind the knees. Bites are intensely itchy. Bites can turn into blisters and hive-like rashes.
- *Prevention*: Avoid people infected at all costs. Don't sleep in open fields or grass without a tarp under you. Practice good hygiene. Use DEET when in grassy areas.
- *Treatment*: Clean yourself with animal shampoo and your belongings. Eat lots and lots of garlic until it is oozing from your skin. This makes your flesh inhospitable. To deal with the itchiness use Calamine, Afterbite, vinegar, honey, vapor rub, deodorant, and thyme essential oil. You can get little packets of honey and vinegar from some fast food restaurants.

Lice

- *Symptoms*: Itchy scalp, tickling feeling of something moving on head or body, irritation, red bumps on head, and appearance of lice eggs on hair shafts
- *Prevention*: Avoid people infected at all costs. Don't share clothing, especially hats, headphones, brushes, and pillows. Clean and comb hair regularly.

- *Treatment*: Wash all your belongings. Wash hair with lice shampoo once every three days for two weeks. Alternately you can cut off hair.

Bed Bugs
- *Symptoms*: Itchy swollen red area with darker red center or raised itchy bump with clear center. The bites can be in a line, zigzagged, or grouped together in small areas around exposed skin. The bites might blister or turn into hives depending on reaction.
- *Prevention*: Avoid sharing beds and clothing. If you share a bed, like in a shelter, place plastic on the bed before laying down. Place all possessions in a plastic bag.
- *Treatment*: Wash all your belongings and dry them on the highest heat. Wash hair and body with lice shampoo. Spread diatomaceous earth (get at Walmart or garden stores) over sleeping areas until all signs of bed bugs are gone. When using, make sure to place on sleeping area and bedding an hour before laying down and then brush it off to prevent inhaling it while sleeping. To deal with the itchiness use Calamine, Afterbite, vinegar, honey, vapor rub, deodorant, and thyme essential oil. You can get little packets of honey and vinegar from some fast food restaurants.

Staph Infection

<u>This can be life threatening</u>

- *Symptoms*: Some signs are redness, warmth, swelling, and pain, as well as painful rash, boils, pustules, scalded skin, blisters, and necrosis (skin cell death).
- *Prevention*: Clean hands often, tend to wounds as quickly as possible, use pads instead of tampons, don't share hygiene items, and wash clothing and self regularly.
- *Treatment*: Wash with soap and water, keep infected area clean and dry, and cover with antibiotic ointment and a bandaid, take Usnea, Echinacea, and Oregon Grape Root tinctures, and eat garlic. If symptoms persist for more than a week or get worse go to the hospital.

Giardia and dysentery

- *Symptoms*: Diarrhea, gas, stomach and abdominal cramping/pain, upset stomach, nausea, dehydration, bloody or greasy stool, fever
- *Prevention*: Don't drink untreated water, wash hands after going to the bathroom and before eating.
- *Treating*: Drink lots of water and rest. In general our immune system will fight it off in a couple of weeks. In the meantime take a dropper full of Black Walnut or Oregon Grape Root tincture 3x's daily. Eat a small amount of

21

charcoal daily – even just burnt bread will help. For diarrhea take dropper full of Blackberry tincture as needed. If symptoms continue for more than a week or worsen, go to the hospital.

You can buy tinctures or you can make them. You can make any tincture just like this Blackberry tincture for diarrhea, just switch the herbs or roots:

- Find Blackberry and dig up its root.
- Clean root with water.
- Chop root into small pieces.
- Place in jar with alcohol (a mini bottle of alcohol like those you get on an airplane work great).
- Allow roots to soak in alcohol for two or more weeks.
- Shake jar daily.
- After a few weeks take out roots and keep the alcohol tincture.
- Take two caps worth when needed.
- Tincture is viable for a year or two.

Trench Foot

Trench Foot is when the feet are constantly moist because of wet shoes and/or socks and they start to get nasty, even gangrene if not treated properly.

- Don't get your shoes wet. If you do, take your shoes to a laundry mat or camp fire and dry them.
- Have an extra pair of socks to put on.

- If feet are bad, stop and take care of them. Clean and dry them, and take care of any blisters and dead spots.
- Let feet dry out as often as possible.
- Don't pop blisters, cover with moleskin or Vaseline and cotton ball.
- Sleep barefooted: no socks.

General Sickness
- Drink lots of water.
- Slow down and get lots of rest.
- Consume vitamin C and Zinc.
- Take dropper full of Oregon Grape Root and Echinacea tincture 3xs daily until symptoms subside or take a tablespoon of Elderberry syrup 3xs a day until symptoms subside.
- Eat garlic.
- Keep warm.
- Go to hospital if symptoms worsen.

Money

Ways to make money
- *Panhandling.* Either ask people for money by saying something like, "Spare some change?" or by sitting down and having a sign asking for money while having a receptacle for people to toss money into. When using this second method it is important to prime the pot, in other words, place some change and a few dollars in your hat, cup, can, or what-have-you.

This increases the likelihood that others will give.

- *Selling things*: This can be flowers, flutes, jewelry, art, or anything else. I knew a guy that sat downtown and made elaborate art on wood with a magnifying glass and the sun. The catch to this is that sometimes you will be chased off by the police for selling without a license.

- *Temp jobs*: Going to temp agencies will work if you have an address, phone, and identification. If you don't have all these things then working at seasonal harvesting jobs, day construction gigs, or things like that are practical options.

- *Playing music*: Playing a flute or some other instrument while having a receptacle for money is a great way to earn a few dollars.

- *Bar tricks*: If going to the bar will put you at risk of relapsing, don't go. If this is not a problem for you, then going to a bar or even sidewalks near a bar and doing tricks is an awesome way to make money. Outside clubs and towns with college kids roaming the streets are also great places to do tricks. Look online for tricks.

- *Selling cigarettes*: While not the most fruitful way to make money, a lot of street people will pay for a cigarette.

- *Selling plasma*: This is a great way to get inside, relax for an hour, and make some money. On average you can make $200 a month doing this.

- *Recycling*: Collect cans. It won't make you rich but it will definitely fill your belly.

- *Door-to-door*: This one is an odd one, but going to different businesses and asking for anything to do will sometimes net you a day's worth of work. Not the most dependable at first, but if you gain a reputation as a dependable person, it definitely starts to pay off.

- *Working:* Get a job. More info on page 27.

Note on panhandling: No matter what method you use to make money, one of the most important things to keep in mind is that no one, not one person is obligated to give you money. With that in mind, be respectful. You are literally asking people to give you free money that they themselves have earned.

Signing

Signing is definitely an art. First and foremost is the message. If the message is too elaborate, if it is written sloppily, if it is unreadable, and if it is insulting, you will fail at making money. The simpler, the better. For instance:

Hungry
Will Work
God Bless

It states something easily addressed: you are hungry and a few dollars can help with that. It states that you are willing to do something for it: you'll work. And it has a religious sentiment that pulls on heartstrings and/or triggers guilt and the desire to give.

As you get better at signing, you can tweak it for your audience. Sometimes being next to a bar and asking for beer money will rake in the money, while being near a comic convention it would be more suitable to ask for money for a Spidey suit. Humor is a great way to make money. If you can write something simple that catches your audience and makes them pause for a moment, you will find yourself making good money. Another thing to consider, if you're needing something specific like a car part or sleeping bag, state that on the sign. I've been given a sleeping bag and other things by just asking for them.

Some places to sign
- Freeway off ramps
- Store exits
- Church exits
- Downtowns sidewalks
- Medians with a light

Once you have your sign and a place to hold it, the next step is presentation. Do not sit there and expect people to throw money at you as they're driving by. Stand up and hold your sign.

The next thing to do is time the light. Spend half of the light walking up the medium or off ramp and the other half getting back to where you started. This adds a little stimulus for the drivers to notice you as well as give them time to think about giving. If you are standing at the very front of the light, most drivers won't even see you until they pass by.

Four helpful things to consider: (1) Have your stuff clearly visible. Sometimes people do not give because they believe the signer is not homeless. Having your bedding and stuff visible eliminates that belief. (2) Stretch and show how uncomfortable you are. If you have been standing and walking for a while, your body will definitely be feeling it. This triggers a sympathetic response that translates into giving. (3) Don't sit there smoking. Why would anyone want to buy your cigarettes? (4) Be positive. I cannot tell you how many times being positive has turned out a better day of earning than when I was feeling bad or had negative thoughts. Singing songs, remembering religious scriptures, thinking of loved ones, or even meditating on the breath while signing makes a difference.

Getting a job

This one can be very hard when on the streets. Some things to consider:

- *Internet access*: Libraries, fast food places, coffee shops, businesses, and some cities have free wifi these days.
- *Address*: Go to UPS or some other company that sells mail boxes with a physical address: don't have a PO Box number. Alternately, if you know anyone with a physical address, ask them if you can use their address.
- *Phone*: Get a free phone. https://www.freegovernmentcellphones.net/states
- *Clothing*: Most thrift stores have a selection of nice clothing and sometimes shoes.
- *Presentable*: Make sure to clean up before your interview. Wash in a sink, shave, comb your hair, make sure you don't smell, clean your teeth, and dress appropriately.

- *Transportation*: City bus and taxi are two options. A third option is to squat near where you work.

Cars

Having a car makes being homeless a lot easier, at the same time it has some disadvantages.

- *Gas*: The easiest way to get gas is to have a sign asking for gas while holding a gas can near the station. It doesn't take long. Other resources are churches and organizations that offer gas vouchers. Usually you can get one or two of these. Just remember to conserve what you have when you can. And if things get really low, panhandle or sign for it.
- *Insurance and tags*: There might be an organization or program in your area that would help with these (look on the internet), for the most part though you will need to figure out how to pay for them. If you can't pay, then you can't pay. Live in your car as long as you can. Try not to drive it and keep it parked somewhere where the expired tags are not noticeable.
- *Driver's License*: There are often programs that help with discounted identification cards, you might find some help paying for your license (look on the internet). As to needing an address, you can either use a local shelter or purchase a mailing address from a UPS store or place like it that gives an actual address instead of a PO Box number.

- *Where to sleep*: This is the best thing about vehicles – almost anywhere. As long as you are discreet, many neighborhoods, around parks, national forests, small highway pull-offs, or Walmart parking lots are all good options to park for the night. *Advice*: make sure not to sleep in the same spot too often, don't sleep in sketchy areas, be quiet, don't trash or stink up the place, and be nice to the officers when they are checking on things and telling you to move on. It happens. Don't be rude. Say sorry and move on.
- *Repair*: some churches and mechanics can help. I've done odd jobs for mechanics to help pay for repairs.

Basic Gear

Try to get as many of these things as you can.

- Sleeping bag
- Tarp
- Tent
- Rope
- Lighter
- P38 or other can opening device
- Knife
- Water bottles
- Extra set of clothes and socks
- Warm clothing/covering and gloves
- Trash bags
- Free phone
- Sharpie marker
- Decent shoes
- Hat or some other shading device
- Hand sanitizer and/or wet wipes
- Toilet paper
- Hygiene stuff
- Ointment and Band-Aids
- Tinctures
- Moleskin for blisters
- Toenail clippers
- Vaseline and cotton balls (good for fire starting and for blisters)
- Rags
- Backpack or means to carry stuff with you at all times

Resources

Write in the numbers, addresses, and times of local resources so that you always have this information with you. You can find most information online by typing in the town you are in and the resource you're looking for.

City Bus (routes and times):

College:

Crisis Hotline: 988

Food and Clothing Banks:

Food/Soup Kitchens (days and times):

DSHS Office:

Gyms:

Hospital:

HUD Housing: (866) 570-8840

Library (days and times):

Mental Health:

Parks:

Police Dispatch:

Shelters:

Thrift Stores:

Churches:

National Hotlines

Alcohol and Drug Hotline (800) 562-1240
Domestic Violence (800) 799-7233
Poison Control (800) 222-1222
Rape Hotline (800) 656-4673
Suicide Hotline (800) 273-8255
Veterans Coalition for Homeless Veterans (800) 838-4357
Youth National Runaway Safeline (800) 786-2929
Physical emergencies call 911
Mental health crisis 988

Psychological Needs

Positive attitude and appreciation
Dignity and Self-respect
Self-care and love
Emotional awareness
Getting enough sleep
Perspective
Anxiety
Future Moving
Choice
Victimization
Social-spiritual relationships
Boredom
Shame and guilt
Suicide
Healing
Happiness

Positive attitude and appreciation: While this can be hard to do, it's worth doing. A positive attitude will likely invite something positive into your life and appreciation will give you a moment of joy. Everyday spend a few moments thinking positive and appreciating things. It will change your life for the better.

Dignity and Self-respect: You deserve to be treated as a human, as a person, we all do. The truth is, you will not always get it. In fact, there will be times when you won't even see it. A friend taught me to reach back into my past and find a moment of strength and hold onto that feeling and experience. Connect with that experience of power and self-respect. Take that

33

experience and build on it. Act in a dignified way and be respectful. Start doing things that feel empowering, that move you in a positive direction, and that increase your state of wellbeing.

Self-care and love: This one is hard even for those that live in homes and work for a living. It's even harder when homeless. My wife taught me that something as simple as a glass of ice water can be self-caring and that even in the depths of despair we can still give love to a puppy, which lets us see how love originates from within us: we need only direct that love towards ourselves to experience it. Do something nice for yourself today.

Emotional awareness: This is another one many people have difficulty with. From a survival standpoint, emotional awareness helps us connect with others and form bonds as well as helps us gain control over our lives instead of being controlled by the emotions. It also helps with self-awareness, self-regulation, and motivation. Start paying attention to how you feel and reflect on it. Is this how you want to feel? If not, what can you do to shift the feeling? What actions and thoughts will change things?

Getting enough sleep: When tired there's more chance of making mistakes, failing to notice things, being irritable, and a host of other issues.

Perspective: You can shift your reality when you shift your perspective. If you're looking for possibilities, you'll find them; if you don't think there are possibilities, you are likely not going to see them.

Anxiety: It sucks. Slowing down, taking calm and full breaths, connecting with the physical sensations of the body, and focusing on something else can all help soften anxiety's hold over you. After that, you have to confront your fears and uncertainties and do something about them.

Future moving: Anxiety, depression, anger, hopelessness, and a host of other unwanted emotions can arise from the feeling of being stuck and powerless. So start making plans and actively move towards them.

Choice: Choice is what ultimately directs your life. Circumstances might arise outside of your control: what you think, say, and do in those situations is up to you. Make conscious choices.

Victimization: Even if you have been victimized, that does not mean you are a victim. In other words, you do not have to hold onto the negative thoughts of being hopeless and helpless. You can choose, are you the "victim or the Victor."

Relationships: Relationships are important because they help you stay safe, feel connected, give support, extend your sense of being, invite happiness, and a host of other good things. Cultivate positive relationships.

Boredom: Who would have thought boredom was an issue? The truth is, without some driving purpose, life can get pretty boring. Hanging out with the same people, having the same conversations day in and out can become quite boring. I suggest doing something. Be that some activity, learning, drawing, journaling, playing music, exercising, having deeper conversations, doing self-introspection, et cetera.

Shame and Guilt: You did something bad – you're not living to your highest potential – you're not being a productive member of society: I get it. What was done is done. This is where you are at now. Be conscious of your choices and act in accordance with your ideals as often as you can from here on out.

Suicide: The fact is, the streets can be very difficult and life can get really dark. Suicide happens all the time. When we add in mental imbalances, drugs, trauma, PTSD, anxiety, fear, depression, and all the other things that come up, suicide starts looking appealing. There are options, you don't have to hurt or kill yourself. Before going down that road I encourage you to call the National Suicide Hotline and talk with someone (800) 273-8255 or the Crisis Hotline 988.

Healing: It is possible. Many people, myself included, have found healing through homelessness. The way I found it was by looking at myself. I did not like everything I saw, but I came to understand myself, and through that, I began to see things I could change. It's not easy. Healing is not just about dealing with symptoms, it's also about changing your behaviors, thought patterns, emotional reactions, consumptions, and beliefs.

Happiness: It's possible too! Once you know how to navigate the streets and create a stable routine, you'll find yourself with a lot of leisure time and little responsibilities to worry about. It's quite freeing. What you do with that time can drastically improve your life. Introspection, appreciating things, learning, building positive relationships, seeking to improve your circumstances, exercising, going to museums on the free days, hanging out in a garden, joining clubs, crafting, and a hundred other things are there for you to do. Whatever you find happiness and joy in, do it. I know someone who work-traded for Belly Dance lessons. If learning the piano or going to the Grand Canyon is what brings you happiness, make it happen. It might not be easy, but it is possible.

Other things I've found helpful in inviting happiness are simplicity, contentment, finding meaning and purpose in life, self-love and kindness, volunteering, connecting with others, meditating and praying, seeing new things, and enjoying life's little things.

May you find shelter, warmth, healing, love, compassion, health, happiness, and wholeness. May you find a place to call Home.

About the Author

Tobias Moore lives in the Evergreen State with his wife and youngest children where he spends a majority of his time homeschooling, playing in the garden, studying, writing, meditating, and giving thanks for life's many blessings.

www.ingramcontent.com/pod-product-compliance
Lightning Source LLC
Chambersburg PA
CBHW030311030426
42337CB00012B/676